More Praise for

Love, Lyric, and Liberation

"It is my honor to remind us to remember, and in doing so reclaim our identity, our culture, and our language. May the Ancestors continue to bless Asantewwaa for showing us how to do this with her words."

Karen Seneferu
artist and curator of "The Black Woman is God"

"Asantewaa has healing powers. She heals through the determination to make us love ourselves regardless of a world that deems us unworthy. She has built infrastructures of community care. She is Yemayaa. Her truth is potent, puncturing hole after hole in this toxic patriarchal, womb stifling, trifling abyss. Her words cut deep in Athena, which seems to be about her infant daughter who died within six months of her mom, 'Though I hoped you'd be a boy so that no one would rape you.' I followed Asantewaa through her life's journeys, from the struggle of losing a child to the concrete street jungle demanding law enforcement stop killing our people. I followed her because she had something to show me, and it fit like a glove. Please read this book, read it to your daughter and son, pick it up when you are unsure and need some healing. Make it a part of your self-care."

Laila Aziz
activist based in San Diego, California

"Asantewaa Boykin's *Love, Lyric, and Liberation* is raw, unapologetic, and beautiful. Her latest work showcases the softer side of rebellion addressing the necessity of self-love and radical joy for those doing liberation work while still naming and confronting injustice with the fearless pen she has come to be known for. A stand-out voice in Sacramento as a community leader, frontline activist, nurse, mother, and poet, *Love, Lyric, and Liberation* is an unabridged collection of thoughts that America should be listening to right now."

Andru Defeye
Poet Laureate of
Sacramento, California (2020–2024)

"Asantewaa's *Love, Lyric, and Liberation* will make you cry, laugh, feel, and think. Her words will make you reflect deeply about what position you take in the war against Blackness, against femininity, against poverty, and against justice. The words in this book will make you question if you are at war with yourself, and if so the book will provide a way for you to find peace.

Love, Lyric, and Liberation is a gift and a treasure. The words in this book are medicine to all the weary freedom fighters, social justice warriors, and Black mothers who struggle everyday to maintain dignity and hope for the voiceless, the powerless, and the innocent Black babies who deserve a genuine opportunity to thrive, to love, and to just be.

Asantewaa's book of poetry offers a scathing critique and assessment of today's current brand of systemic terror against Black bodies. Her words are a weapon and a curse to those who bask in willful ignorance and intentionally stand against justice, love, and freedom for others.

However, her book also provides a blueprint and map for resistance, joy, and healing. Her words are a chisel and the poems exquisite sculptures reflecting both unspeakable pain and unspeakable hope."

Alexandria White
professor of Literature and Language Arts

"Asantewaa Boykin's labor of love to build crisis responses rooted in politicized communities of care through Mental Health First have been an inspiration to thousands of organizers across the country in the context of the 2020 Uprisings. *Love, Lyric, and Liberation* illuminates the forces that underlie this work: the calls of ancestors and future generations, a deep sense of purpose, a profound love for self, children, and community, and a fierce commitment to shape worlds unfolding. This collection of poems and essays from one of the leading voices calling forth a new world affirms that organizing is, fundamentally, an act of love and creation."

Andrea J. Ritchie
author of *Invisible No More: Police Violence Against Black Women and Women of Color*

"This collection of prose and poetry by Asantewa Boykin is a visceral experience of romance and rage, liberation and love. The images and experience hit you in the face with ferocity moving the reader to pain and presence. We must be present to get the message. This collection brings us into a space eye to eye with what moves us; moves us to a place white supremacy can't concede to."

Profesor Jahsun Edmonds

NOMADIC PRESS

OAKLAND

PHILADELPHIA

XALAPA

WWW.NOMADICPRESS.ORG

MASTHEAD
Founding Publisher
J. K. Fowler

ASSOCIATE EDITOR
Michaela Mullin

DESIGN
Jevohn Tyler Newsome

MISSON STATEMENT Through publications, events, and active community participation, Nomadic Press collectively weaves together platforms for intentionally marginalized voices to take their rightful place within the world of the written and spoken word. Through our limited means, we are simply attempting to help right the centuries' old violence and silencing that should never have occurred in the first place and build alliances and community partnerships with others who share a collective vision for a future far better than today.

INVITATIONS Nomadic Press wholeheartedly accepts invitations to read your work during our open reading period every year. To learn more or to extend an invitation, please visit: www.nomadicpress.org/invitations

DISTRIBUTION
Orders by teachers, libraries, trade bookstores, or wholesalers:

Nomadic Press Distribution
orders@nomadicpress.org
(510) 500-5162

Small Press Distribution
spd@spdbooks.org
(510) 524-1668 / (800) 869-7553

Love, Lyric, and Liberation

This book was made possible by a loving community of chosen family and friends, old and new.

For author questions or to book a reading at your bookstore, university/school, or alternative establishment, please send an email to info@nomadicpress.org.

Cover art: "ANCIENT FUTURES" by Asantewaa Boykin RN

Published by Nomadic Press, 111 Fairmount Avenue, Oakland, California 94611

First printing, 2022

Library of Congress Cataloging-in-Publication Data

Title: *Love, Lyric, and Liberation*
p. cm.
Summary: *Love, Lyric, and Liberation* is a collection of reflections, epiphanies, and warnings for those who find themselves existing in the intersection of Blackness, femininity, art, and resistance. These poems and essays pay homage to our ancestors while offering the rest of us a warm embrace.

[1. POETRY / American / African American & Black. 2. POETRY / Women Authors. 3. POETRY / Subjects & Themes / Family. 4. POETRY / Subjects & Themes / Death, Grief, Loss. 5. POETRY / American / General.] I. III. Title.

LIBRARY OF CONGRESS CONTROL NUMBER: 2022934988

ISBN: 978-1-955239-28-8

Love,
Lyric,
and Liberation

Asantewaa Boykin RN

Love,
Lyric,
and Liberation

Asantewaa Boykin RN

**NOMADIC
PRESS**

I'd like to dedicate this collection

to all my past selves

and all your past selves.

May they be showered

with unconditional love,

forgiveness,

and acceptance.

contents

LYRIC

LIBERATION

reading guide

foreword

I remember the first time I saw her with a clarity unusual for the swiss cheese that trauma has made my brain.

A Black August Organizing Committee Meeting in North Oakland when Black folks could still afford to live there. We were an established crew. She was new to the space and entered the room tentatively, but the tornado simmering beneath her humility was palpable.

My first thought when I laid eyes upon Asantewaa Boykin was, "God, she's beautiful ..." I coveted her dark skin and unapologetic Black features. To this, Asantewaa would likely respond with something like, "Bruh, shut up," and giggle. Yes, this warrior for the people, who stares down police riot lines, giggles.

I would soon come to learn that it was more than her features that were unapologetic. So was her love for Black people and her willingness to put her body on the line for our freedom.

For 14 years now, side by side with Asantewaa Boykin, I have organized, built movement, been arrested, shut down highways, blocked traffic, occupied police stations, raised children, built movement and created liberatory institutions and practices that will outlast us both.

But the greatest joy, our sisterly communion and connection, has always been art. Calling, texting, and pulling each other aside in meetings to share words that reflect our rage, pain, passion, and love for our people.

Asantewaa embodies the slogan, "We Take Care of Us." Whether she is providing mutual aid in the middle of an action while flash-bangs and tear gas consume us, teaching community members how to do emergency first aid, raising self care dollars for Black women, developing ground breaking abolitionist programs like MH First, or using the power of the pen to assert and defend the humanity of our people—Asantewaa fights for us.

This book is nothing short of a miracle. Not because sis doesn't have the talent. Talent is literally a strand of her DNA. A miracle because the world has told her, like it's told all of us Black women, we are not worthy, good enough, or deserving. And so we hide, deflect, and diminish ourselves to avoid the trappings of white supremacy which finds our very existence offensive.

I've watched Asantewaa push herself through all that shit, one brave and painful step at a time, to take her rightful place in the literary, artistic, and movement worlds.

And from all that pain, all that emotional effort, all that exorcism, she has birthed this body of work for us. A body of work that allows us to be seen. A body of work that charts a path toward abolition. A body of work that sits firmly at the intersection of arts and activism.

Artists are supposed to be the conscience of our communities. Asantewaa is that conscience. Not just in these words but in her life's work, where she is breaking liberatory ground and slapping white supremacy in the face on the daily.

I am honored to call her sister. Humbled to call her comrade.

She doesn't share herself with just anyone. She guards her essence fiercely and you must prove your worth before she grants even a glimpse.

I'm slightly annoyed that I have to share her with all of you now, while simultaneously thrilled that the world will get to inhale the beautiful, unapologetic, talented, and genius essence of Asantewaa Boykin.

Screw you, capitalism. racism, patriarchy, sexism, inequity, and injustice.

Consider this a warning shot.

We're coming for you. And she is part of the collective Black leadership we follow as we decimate what has been, to forge something new. Something beautiful. Something only artists can help us see.

With her art, activism and advocacy, she has—and continues to—literally changed the world.

Cat Brooks

introduction

On my grandmother's 75th birthday, myself and a few of my cousins decided to create "This is my life" books as party favors for her guests. I knew her as my grandmother and, mostly, as my number one cheerleader. It was at that time, however, that I truly met Bertha, the woman.

Bertha fell in love at a young age and chose that love over Tuskegee University. She spent most of her career as a Domestic Worker and later worked for the "United Domestic Workers Union." When I asked her what she would have wanted to accomplish at Tuskegee, she told me that she wanted to be a writer. Hearing her story helped me understand myself with a sobering clarity. All of my uncles spent a number of years in the military, most if not all of my cousins were college-bound or headed toward long-term careers. And then there was me, an afro-centric, rebel rousing poet, and the literal "Black Sheep." I was not only the most melanin-rich of all of my cousins but also, in my opinion, the most odd. A small stint in juvie, an artistic band, and an obvious obsession for the road less traveled. Writing for me always came naturally, and after being introduced to the real Bertha, I now know why. Publishing this book is in appreciation of all of the sacrifices that she made to raise my mother, who raised me.

Like my grandmother, my mother's wholeness was a mystery. It wasn't until my mother's golden years, and more so after she died, that I became aware of the dynamic woman she was. Valerie had spent some time in Tacoma, Washington, doing something that no one talks about. She also spent some time with an unnamed Black Power organization. Of these things she was the least candid about her time as a go-go dancer.

Valerie was not a religious woman but she took very careful care of Hijab and the Quran and one day boldly informed me that, "Malcolm X was a traitor and not a Freedom Fighter." I still wonder how she fell in love with a Baptist sailor from the midwest. Valerie loved and cared for every person who crossed her path. She helped raise her four brothers and countless cousins. Sometimes her love was hard, other times it was soft but it was always passionate. If Valerie loved you, she loved you with her whole self and would fight for, with, and beside you. Without a doubt, I Am my mother's daughter.

No matter where I find myself on the globe, or what role I am fulfilling—nurse, activist, mother, wife, auntie, friend, or foe—my pen and paint brushes are always present. Outside of the arms of my mother and her mother, the process of creating is where I feel safest. In these pages you will find a piece of my soul, the creative expression of my brightest and darkest moments. You will find written evidence of a journey to discover my own wholeness so I can share that wholeness with my children, their children, and yours. With the hope that they will never have to hide their wholeness from themselves or anyone else.

Love, Lyric & Liberation is, quite literally, the manifestation of my ancestors' wildest dreams.

Asantewaa Boykin RN

"No revolutionary movement is complete without its poetic expression."

James Connolly

LOVE

That's Love

I love niggas
Like southeast
Like rolled tacos with cheese
The brown padre hat
With the orange SD
Like
Marcus Garvey
Like runaways looking for North Stars
Or Black Stars
Searching for self
I love niggas
Like triggers love fingers
And nooses love necks
And my mama loved me
And me

Athena

I love niggas enough to oppose an enemy with
100 guns against my one
And still fight
Enough to live
And heal
Despite the urge
To trust salty seas
Instead of unknown shores
Enough to love Black

Live Black
Die Black

And shine golden like
The tips of pyramids
Diamond studded grills
And sunsets off the coast of Ghana

I love niggas

Like

Nehanda loved niggas
Enough to take niggas
To meet niggas
Who never knew chains
So they could unshackle their own
And love
This sun-kissed brilliance we call skin

I love niggas enough to feel the pain
Soak the lashes
Suture the gunshot wounds
Breathe life into stolen wombs
And the dark mental abysses that cry for freedom
With the faith it takes to wait for Jesus
When we know

That nigga's
Not
Coming

And the gumption to run
When the time comes
I love niggas
Enough

                            To leave

Summah y'all niggas

                            Behind

And still
Ask the ancestors to watch over you
Until
We meet again
On this plane or the next

My Nigga,

                                                  I Love you

Love

You
Me
Us
Him
Her
Her
And the one with no name
Curious this love thang
I was blindsighted
Despite looking right at you

In awe of your endlessness

Baffled at your brilliant contradictions
Fully aware of exactly why you love me

And you

Knowing
I need that

Thank you for not believing the lies
I tell myself
Challenging the honesty
In us both
You shine so brightly

And require
The same of me

My grass is greener
My juices sweeter

I'm better
Because of you

For us
Her
Her
Him
And the one with no name

Be Kind To Yourself

We can be our own worst critics. This goes without saying. For those of us who carry the weight of the world on our shoulders our failures not only affect ourselves, but also the people/institutions we serve.

2015 was a rough year. Rebellions were happening all over the country in response to the murder of Mike Brown, I had just finished nursing school, enduring fertility testing and treatment, and my mother was growing increasingly ill. Between frequent trips back home, meetings on top of meetings, direct actions and studying for Nursing Boards, life felt heavy. In the midst of all this unrest and uncertainty, joy came. I was pregnant. The studying continued. Direct action continued. My mother's condition didn't improve, but there was new life happening. Unfortunately, my daughter was born at 23 weeks and didn't survive and my mother passed 6 months later. I had resolved that they wanted to be together as ancestors. Though comforting, this resolution came after many tears and much struggle. At some point during this fog of grief I remember being told, "be kind to yourself." Though I don't remember who said it, I will never forget those words.

As simple as it sounds it had never occurred to me. In my activism and studies I had extensively contemplated and articulated things like Justice, Equality, Power, Fairness, and Equity, but not Kindness. I knew what it meant to be kind to my patients and how to show compassion for victims of police terror and their families. Kindness as a self-directed act was foreign.

I was grieving. I was not only grieving the loss of my loved ones but grieving the realization the future I spent my life fighting for may not actualize in my lifetime. But in the midst of that grief, I began considering kindness. I had become skilled at crafting narratives in my head that sounded like, "That was sloppy, do better," "I'll sleep when I die," or, "No one cares how you feel, get it done." I came to understand that this narrative was not kind. When these narratives reared their ugly heads I'd ask myself, "Would I say this out loud to anyone else?" If the answer was no, then with mindful intention and practice, I had to remind myself that I did not cause my daughter's death. I had to remind myself I had been a good and present daughter to my mother and that I had done my best, because I always do.

This simple action changed the relationship I had with the memories of my mother and daughter. It also changed how I operate in relation to movement work and the folks I worked with. I began to sit on memories of me and my mother laughing or cooking together. I remember the moment that I told my daughter that this life was hers and for her to do with it what she chose. I dwelled on the victories we won for the people instead of the things we have yet to do. I began to offer my comrades compassion and not just accountability.

With that said, my loves, "Be Kind to Yourself." After all, in the end we are all motivated by love. Love for our people. Love for the people we serve. Love for the folks we work with. Love for our families and friends. In order to truly love them all we must also love ourselves.

–Ase

For Athena

I know that you'll be intelligent
Quick-witted
And even quicker with the lips
Perhaps a little sarcastic
I imagine you won't be able to help it
Im hoping your presence
Will make my patience a little longer
And hands a little slower
Because now I know children are not to be controlled
But firmly guided

I pray you're wise
And even if you choose to do what you believe you shouldn't
Be woman enough
To accept the consequences

Be fearless
Realize that your reality is

What *You shape*

And all these rules are just

Cages

And bitch is not a pet name
And bitch is not a pet name

Me and your father will be the first to tell you
You're great
But be the first to convince yourself of it
I love you
Never get off the phone or leave the presence of the ones you love
Without saying
I love you
You'll never regret it

I loved you

Before creation saw fit to plant you in my womb
And long before your father wooed me
I loved you
Though I hoped you'd be a boy
So no one would rape you
Or tell you
You're ugly so fervently that you would believe them
So you wouldn't have been born on the bottom of the
white male
patriarchal
totem pole*

Beloved, have the courage to scream FUCK YOUR POLE then burn
that bitch slowly

Mommy cusses–ALOT

Be soft enough to forgive
So pain doesn't weigh you down like anchors
And I know you will find this hard to believe, my little pea

9

You were not BORN a queen
But a crown is not far from your reach
So go get it
Be kind
Especially to yourself
Never mind the naysayers, even if it's Me
Your father will always say, "No"
But give him a minute
He'll change his mind
And remember

We love you

* Totem poles are sacred statues used mostly by North Western First Nations Peoples. These statues are used to document lineage and significant historical events. In this western colonized culture, the term "totem pole" is used to describe one's placement inside a hierarchical system. I acknowledge the use of the term in this poem does not reflect the sacredness of our Indigenous siblings traditions. The intended context speaks to the perversion of Indegenous cultures by colonizers and our embodiment of that perversion.

Cautionless

Your love caught my
Left brain case
Killed logic
The right way
Slow
Bled out prettier
Than white women
On benzos with slit wrists
In porcelain tubs

Pretty in pink

Chocolate encased lips
Just the way you like it

Poetic, just the way you love it
I love it

Swimming down an endless canal
Of cautionless winds

I can paint the stars from here
Unlock bars from here
Lick wounds
Move mountains
Conquer worlds
And hear

Everything

The birds and trees
Earthworms breathing

Temporal lobe neglected
Left to ponder direction
While the rest of me just went
But you never let me follow
And you
Too determined to be lead

So we marched
down unexplored roads together

Never holding hands
Just the unbelievers at bay
If rainbows ended you would place the potted gold
At my feet
And grin
As I returned the favor

Until we decided to birth ideas
Instead of treasures
Peace instead of grudges

Honest intent instead of misinterpreted actions

The graceful statement of gratitude
Could never be enough

Anxiety

Tired
Can't sleep
Restless
Can't breathe
I keep checking to see if you're breathing
Yet

The rise and fall of his chest
Brings no relief

Trying to balance

Joy
            and

Grief

The reality
                and
Disbelief

Psalms of Brujas 5

Perhaps
We are all just trying to ditch
These bodies
Escape the weight of 'em

Subconsciously aware
That this plane has
No permanence
Not even the plane itself

Untitled

The taste
Of
Ocean breeze
Reminds me

No one truly dies
Until they elect not to return
So until we meet again, my love
Either here
On salty earth
Or
In that final resting place among
The stubborn or wise
I pray you learn
Suffer less

Shine

Find your back bone quicker than I
And experience the kind of love
That lures you back to flesh
Over and over again

Perhaps our paths will cross
And share something
Felt and unspoken

Choices

For those of us who know

      Suicide

            Is always
On the table

Those who have made love
To our darkest thoughts
In broad daylight

To those who've choked Death's
Throat chakra
And screamed in its place

Let us be
            Patient

For those of us whose breast bones
Find the floor
Before
Our knees
May we muster the energy
To find our
Feet
If only
In this particular moment

For we
Love
As intensely as
We hurt
We fight
As briskly as
We run
We drown our sadness in bottles, zig zags, on the laps of bodies with
unknown names, in movements, on lost souls, or in hollow pools
filled with leeches

Dying slow in hopes to forget
While being willing to die
So
We're not forgotten
Remember
Breathing
                        Is on the table too

Untitled

I
Imagine me
Imagining you
Waiting
Not
Long
But patiently
For me
To walk in
Just to wonder if
I am
The reason
For your smile

Some years ago, I remember walking up to a registration table for a Black August Celebration where Carroll and Cat were sitting with their daughters, Jaydn and Luna. I wasn't sure if I should back out slowly or offer loving hugs. Most notably, I remember not being able to distinguish which child belonged to which woman. I knew I wanted to experience parenthood this way, and had experienced a similar childhood. We had brothers, sisters, cousins, uncles and aunties who we loved yet shared no blood with. Some of our parents were lost to addiction, been incarcerated, or were otherwise unable to provide for short or extended periods of time. Those extended family relationships were formative to my ideas of what it means to raise children.

Over the years, both Cat and Carroll saw me through some of the most joyous and painful periods in my life. Specifically, the birth of both my children and the transition of my first born, Athena. I without a doubt know both women hold a piece of her with them in their hearts, and for that I am eternally grateful. In turn, I've had the privilege of watching them raise brilliant, free, self-determined Black children. I hope, for those children, I am their artistic/hippie Titi they can paint with, talk acrylic nails with, or debate the complexities of rap lyrics with, knowing that no matter what happens—anywhere or ever—that they will always have a safe place to land.

In their own way these women both taught me, either by example or by direct confrontation, about the complexities of what it means to be: Black, woman, and mother, specifically in the setting of dismantling white supremacy. One might come to the conclusion that the conditions we live under as people/women of color makes these "informal" familial structures necessary. Others might argue that these "informal" familial structures are in fact normal and natural, especially when compared to other non-white familial structures all over the globe. No matter which side of this argument is most true, these structures have saved lives, kept some of us out of foster care, out of the psychiatric facilities, and provided systems of care that can not be found in "traditional" care systems.

I wrote this poem to honor them, to honor our respective mothers, and their mothers, and their mothers. To honor our respective and collective children, specifically our respective and collective daughters, and those daughters to come. I wrote this poem to honor the collective sacrifices that were made to make it easier for us and our children to not only imagine what freedom tastes like, but to hopefully one day savor it.

From Cages

for Carroll Fife & Cat Brooks

We are raising
Free babies

From cages

Carving maps and scales
In concrete walls
And
Blue skies from stone

We named them after stars, constellations and
Ancients
So when lost they can find their way back

We pave their roads with blood
Marking landmines along the way
Whispered affirmations as they slept

Some of us
Androgynous
Gender bending out of necessity
Without the *privilege* of either

Filing diligently at steel bars
Until our nails broke
And palms were sore

We hid freedom songs in lullabies
Wisdom in wives' tales
Survival skills in parables
And vowed to tell them the truth
Even
       When
            It
                Hurts

We lose sleep watching their

Breath

And lose our own
Watching them

Leave to expand the engraved maps

We left them

To the ones
       We bore

For the ones who
       Bore us

Both
Extended and blood
My loves
Be free

Intuition

Luckily love lives above the waist
Unfortunately below the brain
It quivers in our guts
Quickens the heart
Narrows the throat
Spouting words
We wouldn't otherwise said
It burns bridges that light the way
To anonymous places
We eventually
Call home

Lessons

You
Are like the one who got away
But
Came back
Like a wayward lover
Leaving me
Cold
But

Wiser

It's like you knew

Like he knew

In order to
Understand
The words I painted
I had to taste them
Like tear gas on my
Tongue
Like blisters
On my
Feet
Like knowing
That I don't know
And what I do

I do
Because
I got licks and scars to prove it

Psalms of Brujas 12

"Space"

I pray my spirit rest
Somewhere between
A bullet-proof vest
And flesh
That space between
Paint brush
And
Canvas
I hope one of my poems
Finds its way
Into the hands
Of a 16-year-old South American
Girl holding down the tail end
Of a migrant caravan
Conjuring daydreams
Of
What it means to be both femme
And militant

That's it
That all in
Blacksmith
Fire born
The

Fuck that
"I am the storm"
The rush between
The cock back
And the fist
Landing

If and when
I'm ever remembered
Let it be in the form
Of that internal
Whisper that gives us the courage to go

Psalms of Brujas 3

She be
Busy counting
Stars and sheep
Decoding algorithms
Without end
Knowing
Earth can't
Be flat
Cause her belly
Round?

In
Addition time and space
Though a continuum
Could never be linear
Cause her crown is coiled
Which means her time is

Had been

And will forever

Be now

An Ode to Oakland

I pray your murals
Never fade
Or fall victim

To your opposed newness

Intersections

Tattooed
Like crop circles

Evidence of
Our fearlessness

I hope 7th St
Becomes something similar to what
Our ancestors remember

May the seeds planted by Monroe's babies
Grow tall and shade the sacred spaces
Where Ohlone bodies lay

May the same spirit of resistance
That drew me back to Drucella's frontier
Continue to inspire the world
To be bold
Non-compliant

And creative

May these streets remain yours
That Black and Brown folks remain beautiful and present
Without the elitist illusions
That keep us from reaching GOD
May we speak the same language

From 106th and Mac to 10th and Wood
May the same soil that grounded all ten of my toes
And shattered the concrete that bound both my wings
Forever
Flourish
Glimmer
Create
Throw molotovs
Scream "Fuck The Police"
Free dragons
Find flight on four wheels
In pure defiance
Always be fertile

LYRIC

Treble Clef
& A Whole Note

Mesmerizing melodies
And
Medicinal drum beats
Maestro mutter pleasure upon our ears

We dance
Conjuring
Spirits with our movements
As fluid as
The fluid
We depend on
To live
Change
Transition

It shapes
Ideas A
Perceptions
Ideology

It's almost policy

Check out my crates
Tape deck
CD's

iPod
My Spotify playlist

It's obvious

I'm a steel drum
Nina Simone
Mitchy And Talib
Kind of
Chick

Positive affirmations blasting
Loving self remastered to perfection
Car doors knockin' warrior calls
On Gawd
I have *surrendered*
When my hands raise

In agreement
With a head nod

Caught in a trance
When my fingers snap

Odd

First heard Assata's name
In a song
Looked it up
Read the book

My mother was alive during that time
So I asked some questions

The answers
Put poems in perspective
Taught me to seek
Rhyme schemes
That matched my tones
Each break and beat

Crescendoed bridge
From
        them
                to
                        us
                        From
                us
        to
Them

It's music

Bleed

I want to bleed on you
Scream on you
Fuck you
Kill you
Make love to you
Leaving you lonely
Mourning my memory
But
You make
Many men
Feel like kings
So
      I'll share you
But

While you're mine
You're my slave
Bend to my will
Make patrons
Call my name
Brave
Shit
God like
Your light
Makes my melanin pop
And dries tears
Yet

Even, with all the applause
We are
Merely men

And

You
Wood with nails
Cords and microphones
So while we're here
I own you

Metaphysical Make-Up of Kendrick Lamar

Let's talk about the metaphysical make-up of Kendrick Lamar
And
Whether or not
2pac was resurrected in his lyrics
Let's talk about whether or not the Koch brothers are sitting in pyra-
mid-shaped temples
Openly discussing
The destruction of the Black Man
Because
For centuries now
They have been the white sheep

That's deep ...

Why is it that every carcinogenic substance known to man is absolutely legal
While phoenix tears, ayahuasca and LSD are not
And
Really?
Was everyone partying Dec 31st 1999?
Or were they drowning their sorrows in liquor
While secretly hoping to die
And do doves cry
I mean really cry

If not
They can't actually be a representation
Of love
Because that -ish hurts
Like a needle in the eye
Or like a camel through the eye of a needle
And is that a real place?
A metaphor?
Or both?

Speaking of Jesus

Is he Black?
I mean...
Really Black?
Is Jesus African?

Does Jesus look like Kendrick Lamar?

Not the clean cut ready for the Grammys " Mr. Lamar"
But the nappy-headed nigga sitting on top of a 64
A half mile from Leimert Park
Right in the heart of Compton, La'Mar

If you ask me
I think Jesus is a she

And so was his father
Who I bet a million dollars wasn't a virgin
But did have two things
White supremacy can't concede to

Clean

Call me clean
Like 20-inch spheres
Pure
Like the uncut
They were purchased with
Call me queen like
Nanny, Asantewaa, or Latifah
Call me
Cold
Like slim frozen fresh water masses
Massive
Like aerosol murals painted
By deities with names unknown to man
Or by the name my mother gave me
The one my father forgot
That I changed
Call me Ase, Amen, Inshallah
Call me damned
Defiance
Call me resistance
Rebel
Hellfire
A pawn in games
Where pawns defeat kings
And Kings are barefoot paupers
In deserts with no bread
Call me human

Hue?
Maaaaaan...
Call me
"Blaque"
Like bat-lined water falls
On dark continents
We now call Mama

Free

Call us liberated
Past tense
If not for us, then for unclaimed souls
Whose names should be
Art
Not war

Psalms of Brujas 4:1

I'm not royalty

Bitch

I'm omnipotent

Don't believe me
Ask Jesus
We with
That
Shit
Like hurricanes with
Slave names
Cracka, fuck yo bricks
Won't be no auctions today
Hoe, we'll sink this ship

Psalms of Brujas 4:2

My mama made miracles
With two pairs
Of draws
And three of them had holes in 'em
What you know about magic?

She caught bullets with her booty
Hid golden stools in her pussy

She was electricity
Her trauma was Tookie

Cause there's just some things
You can't undo

Like blackberry stains on pavement.

And reflections tainted by Maybelline

Resurrected
By
My Aunt Lillie Mae's
Lean in them heels

Over yonder

In promised lands

Made for those with weary feet to rest.

Psalms of Brujas 4:3

This
Should be said in language
That is widely understood

FUCK THAT

No more room for you on sidewalks
Or narrow corridors
Built only for those who

Fit
In
To your narrow
Definitions of normal
No more cages
No more caving to standards
We can't stand for
No more participation in systems that
Systematically
Treat our very existence like a fucking disease
No more pleases and thank yous
Just

Machetes

High heels

Power Grabs

And pretty Black hips
Skipping down bloody
Unoccupied roads

Destination unknown

A collision with my own
Divinity

Long overdue

Some Call You God

Some call you God

If so
Heed my prayers
Take note of my immortal admiration

Some say
You are savage
But even if you rob, kill, and take of mens' flesh
Please
Leave my innocence intact

Some say
You *fancy, flashy, savvy, clever,* resilient
If so then
Sprinkle me mane'

They say you're lost
Father's gone, mother's bitter, brother's dead or dying slow in mental and
concrete caskets
Yet none have deemed you weak, extinct, nor incapable
So fill their bellies and be better than your father
Tack your brilliance to their doubts like GOD has stars across infinite skies

Vastness

Wrapped in endless

Potential
Please excuse me as I clench
And ponder on whether or not it is sacreligious
How the thought of God
Turns me on

16 Bars

16 bars of fire
To melt the mic

16 bars of heat
To make it hot

She drop
16 bars of truth
To bring the light

16 bars of fire
Melted the mic

16 bars of psychological scars
Beat through
10-inch-thick
Walls
Of insecurities

While on the other side
The
World
Waits
For their virgin minds
To be penetrated

By

This society's perception of urbanality

Now me and you both know

URBANALITY

Is not a word

But
It's cool if you can
Get away with it

Cause now-a-days
There are no rules
Go on
My nigga
Do what you do

Long as PoPo
Don't get ya
Cause
Now-a-days
They
Ain't
Passin'
Out life sentences
They split you

In the head

Leave you

For dead

Which
Doesn't sound so
Bad
Heard they got mansions
Up there in heaven

Now see
What
16 bars will get ya

16 bars of fire
To melt the mic
16 bars of heat

To make it hot

She drop 16 bars of truth
To bring the light
16 bars of fire
Melted the mic

2010

Poems are flowin'
Like automatic gunfire
Keepin' hot slugs comin'
Like OPD in a ceasefire
Words appointed by the most high
Who's bound by no sky
No name
No imperialist reign
No orthodox cage
Nor printed words on a page
My prophet turned over tables
In temples
And brought thought gods
Down off their pedestals
So fear me
Like cowards do
Death
Like the establishment
Fears unrest
And niggas do
Revolution
Synthesized drums polutin' your minds
Leaving the upright spineless
So that even serpents stand tall
Mama used to say if only these walls could talk
I once thought that impossible
But then I saw a pig

Stand on two and walk
So I believe in phenomenon
Occasionally taking time
To
Listen to the walls
Cause apparently
Those before us
Thought they'd have something to say
And we got something here to do
Other than pray
It's no use in having callus knees
And baby soft feet
Faith is to action
What placentas are to birth
What the Sun
Is to the Earth
Like 1 is to 7
Like what I am to you
Like a bullet without
A gun
There's not much you can do
8 steps ahead of the game
7 degrees above boiling
All 6 senses in check
And only 5 percent of y'all
Are still listening
And if only we could
Transcend beyond
Preaching
And all these motivational
Monologues

That run on to absolutely nowhere
In search of rainbows
And golden staircases leading to Zion
While our babies are still crying
Politicians are still lying
And people are still starving
Cause I read
David didn't pray
He took a slingshot to Goliath
His index
God manifested in flesh
Movement at its best
The taste of turtle dust on an
Arrogant hare's lips

Psalms of Brujas 10

"Divinity"

My eyes have seen men
Fight men
And cage the
Men they've beaten
Tear gas
Burns eyes
Focused on freedom
Babies die
Women scream
I've seen poor men
Give poor men
Bread to eat
Clothes to keep
Warm
Knowledge
And books to read

Beauty
Amongst the ugliest of things
Treachery deep in the souls of those
Thought to be most beautiful

If no God exists
May we find divinity in each other

Psalms of Brujas 11

"Pussy"

Pussy
Pimping power moves
No pun intended
Sister
Use what you got
Crevice
And the power of creation
Let them be
Mad

Shame your nature
Fuck 'em and feed 'em
Fish
After all
They love it

Fight

Clit
Teeth
And nail
Plant your placentas
Adjacent to sage
And your dead babies

At prison gates
And pray they rain damnation
Like Gods they are ....
Invert your c-section scars to monuments
Of resistance

Fire next time
And mean it

Intersections

I like
Hip-Hop by
Old heads
Returned souls
I need my lyricist
To have survived
A knock
A couple of notches
A gunshot wound
Or two

Third eye open
Other two
Optional
But that's
Seven
Then again
So is God
You know
Hotep niggas
The ones who paved
The road
So y'all could plant
Roses in intersections
But you don't
Hear me though
The ones who understand evolution

Rolled with it
But don't forget
Home
Put political climate
In context
Over samples
The vinyl kind
So you feel it in your soul
1 Part soapbox preacher/pimp (same shit)
3 Parts Black power
2 Parts hood nigga
1 Part contradiction
But then again that's seven
And you don't hear me though

Psalms of Brujas 1

This pussy squirts stardust
Elements dripping from my breast
Sodium, magnesium, and potassium on my breath
Drunk on polynucleotide chains
Relaxing in vastness
Feet kicked up on Saturn
Nape nestled on Mercury
3rd eye aligned with the Sun
We are
She is
Just a fraction
The variable and common denominator
Of unknown nothings
Attracting answers
To questions
Unasked

Psalms of Brujas 2

She's surrounded by sage and crystals
Mid pendulum swing
Chalked Adinkra symbols and moon cycles
Breathing into her
Root chakra
Saying
"Don't worry we'll find it"
While trying to balance
Trauma and sin
On the callus of her left pinky toe
Her strongest
Limb
Only to understand that shame outweighs them both

LIBERATION

Una Voz
De Mujer Sabia

I heard an old woman say
It's about time for revolution
She could smell it in the air
Between the stench of exhaust pipes
And cigarette smoke

She said,

Watch the clock
On history's wall
Go
Tick-Tock

Watch the lifeless bodies
Our babies falling

One
By
One
By
One

They're getting tired
No more
Airbrushed t-shirt

Memorials
Or black ties
And
The summers are hotter
Now
The tides are rising
Their eyes are widening

Rising up
One
By
One
By
One

It's about time
For revolution, she said
Do you hear the battle cries
Drums fading in the wind
The trembling fear of our enemies
Knowing once and for all they've
Underestimated their captives

I got a pamphlet from an army recruiter,
She said
Remembering the last draft
Killed two of her sons

And the one that remains
Resides in a cage

These times are familiar,
She said

I hope to be present
When the patient
Lose what little patience
They may have left

When songs
Of solidarity
Drown out the sound
Police sirens
And helicopters

She remembers
The rainbows of fists
Lifted aggressively in the air
Her great grandmother
Telling tales of that fateful day in June when
Freedom became thiers

The disgusted stares of ghost-like men
Who wanted her dead
But didn't know why

It's time.

"Suspect"
in Custody

A mostly Christian
Otherwise well mannered
Yet somewhat disturbed
White male
With possible mental health issues
You know
The loner type
An Insane Clown Posse fan
Or
A tortured soul radicalized by demon Islamist
His mother was a school teacher
I mean
Who would have thought

Right?

After all those
Racist posts
Posing with guns
Blatant threats
Previous cases
Notes from the Principal
His therapist
His Mama
I mean

Who would have thought

Right?

That all this beautiful, righteous infallible whiteness
Would fail us so miserably

Yet the mere existence of my Blackness is a threat
The mere existence of my son's flesh
Is a threat

Justifiable homicide
For walking while eating Skittles in a hoodie
For running away
For being fucking
Facedown and handcuffed
Or forgetting
That her Black girl rage had no place in their jailhouse

If I could lose this skin
I might
If I could jump this ship
And face the sharks I might
And I might
And some
Do
And some did
Others will

Still

Who could comfort their inconsolable
Mothers

Rather they be the victims of otherwise decent white men

Or the victims of
White supremacist
Henchmen

Yet there's not enough
Salt in our tears
To wash it away
Or to mask the subtle
Reminders
That the scales will
Never tip in our favor

Do not be deceived ...

While those of us who are poor and disenfranchised scrape by with 1% of this country's wealth, it is my hope that we not allow ourselves to be pinned against each other by those who would benefit from our division. As I write, I am reminded of a parable. A parable about a group of people who spoke the same language (which I interpret as being unified), who because they were unified decided to build a tower to reach god. As they neared their goal, god decided to scatter them across the globe and make them speak different languages so they would not make such a mistake again. To me, this is an example of what humans with clear points of unity have the ability to accomplish if we speak the same language or are unified.

First, the talking heads tell us the average white person is secretly (or not so secretly) racist, Black folks are uneducated and/or predators, our Lantinx siblings are illegal and have stolen our jobs. The talking heads tell us that poor people are lazy and that anyone who works hard enough can be wealthy and "successful." Some of us are liberals or conservatives, others independent or radical. Some of us are criminals while others are law-abiding citizens.

Meanwhile, the cost of healthcare, housing, and food keeps rising. Drug addiction and poverty have plagued our communities, water quality in some places isn't fit for human consumption, smoke from wildfires is clogging our lungs, Black folks are still being murdered by police, the educational cost is still too high, while entry-level positions remain few and far between.

Meanwhile, business for those who control the resources is good, the market fluctuates but remains stable, private prisons are the new gold rush, defense contracts are plenty, given capitalism's unending appetite, there will surely be more to come.

So we have found ourselves divided by race, class, gender, sexual orientation, political ideology, and party.

As Babylon crumbles before our eyes fueled by the greed and the arrogance of white supremacy and those who uphold it.

It is my hope that we remember this country was built for and by wealthy white male land/corporation owners and their immediate white male descendants. If you do not fit into that category then, yes, my friend, it is white supremacy's goal to use your labor, body, intellectual, and artistic capacity for its own benefit.

White supremacy is not a respecter of persons. For those who have been awarded privilege by this white supremacist system, understand, you are not safe. Once niggas, poor people, criminals, and so-called "aliens" have been done away with, it will surely come for you.

Psalms of Brujas 8

"West"

The wind has blown west
Stealing her breath
Ripping her seed from her chest

Leaving mother alone to cry
One by one
She waved her children goodbye
Africa has mourned our departure
Our torture
Our slaughter

She's asked her brothers and sisters
To welcome her refugee children
Puerto Rico
Jamaica y Cuba

She wonders why
We've become so complacent
Leaving her waiting
To once again nourish her stolen seeds

The wind has blown west stealing her breath
Ripping her seed from her breast
Never again to be seen

4/30

Sirens blare guns blast
Innocent men die as boys
The motives unchanged

Sirius P

So what happens
When spaceships become
Slave ships
And
White supremacy
Pimps
Interstellar travel
The same way it did
The Mayflower
When Earth becomes
Africa
And
Africa's
Forgotten
Would you trade me
For
Fancy space fabric
Stardust
Or
Moon rocks

Did we save our pennies
To send our babies
To Martian Universities
So they can learn about how history
Repeats itself
Hypothesizing on why

Earthlings are the new niggas
And why are there so many niggas
In zero gravity prisons

Meanwhile trigger happy
Pigs in rocket boots are still
Killing niggas

Both new and old

So we clog traffic on Saturn's rings
In protest
Proclaiming to fight differently
Than our
Earthbound ancestors

Looking back to earth for answers
Instead of futher into the stars
Terraforming loopholes
Charting anomalies that allow us
To break cycles
So we can
Dream
And see
Beyond our conditions
Further than our fingertips
Light years past the length of our legs
And whatever surface they're
Attached to
                         If they're attached at all

Police in Healthcare

Imagine it's 2 AM. and after a night of drinking, you stumble and cut your elbow on a piece of glass. Even in your drunken stupor you realize that this "son of a cut" needs stitches, so off to the ER you go. Before ever seeing a nurse or a doctor, the first face to greet you is one of a police officer. Imagine being stitched up and on your way home, said officer inquires about what happened, how did you get here, and so on.

Those of us born in Black bodies are familiar with the flutter, the racing thoughts and flashbacks that occur when a police officer asks to speak with you. We are acutely aware that our Blackness has already made us guilty of being a potential menace. Yet under all this duress for survival purposes it is in our best interest not to appear nervous or guilty. After all, we just came to the hospital for some stitches.

As a nurse I have seen law enforcement and prison guards leave intubated patients handcuffed to hospital beds, and we all, or most of us, have heard about women in prison giving birth in chains.

When did we as health care providers give up? When did we surrender one of our most essential systems up to the prison industrial complex and the henchmen that fuel that beast? The need to feel safe is understandable. Creating an environment that is safe for some and not all, is not.

So what happens when someone finds themselves assaulted, shot, stabbed, suicidal, or when a victim of domestic violence finds themself in need of medical attention? What happens when their fear of law enforcement feels more overwhelming than their injuries? Will the domestic violence victim be pressured into giving information that will result in more physical abuse later? Will an easily treated wound become infected and cause further and possibly systemic harm? Will our suicidal patient complete suicide because death seems more bearable than jail?

Police in their various forms are in our schools from elementary to university, hospitals, transit systems, they are at our borders, in our airports and skies. Where official police forces do not reside, we have the type of security forces whose agenda is clearly to protect property and not people.

We have to begin to ask ourselves, what are we afraid of? And are we so afraid that we are willing to compromise our practice, our oaths and integrity, for a system that has historically and systematically oppressed, murdered, and harmed the very people we have sworn to care for?

The Florence Nightingale pledge ends by stating, "I will devote myself to the welfare of those committed to my care." There are many parts of that pledge that are problematic and outdated but not this part. If we as nurses, doctors and healthcare workers are truly committed to the welfare of our patients, then creating an environment where ALL of our patients feel safe should be our priority.

There is an historic mistrust of the healthcare system by POC, queer, poor, addicted folks, and folks with mental health needs. This distrust is further fueled by having uniformed and armed police at our front doors.

We must diligently guard against our hospitals and clinics becoming a part of America's growing police state. We do not have to grant police access to our patients or their health information. We can inform our patients of their rights, we can challenge policies, culture, and practice in our respective hospitals and clinics. We can organize and demand not to work in an environment where guns are being openly carried by *anyone*. We can demand that medical attention should be given when necessary and not when police deem a situation "safe."

No matter what our political party, religious beliefs, or life experiences, we can agree that our patients should not be afraid to walk through our doors.

Goddess Wrath

If God is a woman
Black like me
Trauma deep
Womb a shallow grave
Exterior beaten
Bloody
Internally
Conflicted
With little hope for reconciliation

Then pray

But then again
To whom?

Lay your sacrifices of hollow promises
Pegasus and pipe dreams
At my altar of miracle meals and steady roofs

That I may take the sanctified flesh
Of
My demonized babies down from your concrete crosses
Unlock their steal cages
Undo the damage
Of them not knowing that they mama was all knowing

If God is Black
And woman
Like me
I'd be afraid
Scared that Yemaya and Oya
Would recruit their bravest
To render good ol' fashion righteous wrath

Or is god the woman
The one who is Black
Like me
Not postured for vengeance
Just quietly hidden behind
Peaceful veils
Of endless nourishment
Forgiveness and swag

Missed Call

Hello, higher self
I saw you called
But
My ringer was off
Been a little consumed with
"To do" list
And measuring my worth
Against Facebook posts.
Holding grudges
Eating pain
Avoiding confrontation
Is a full time job
So I hope you can be patient
Cause I ain't
Yet
I find myself self waiting
On Gods I don't believe in
And a system that doesn't
Affirm me
To doordash bags of justice and salvation

If you're not too busy
I could pencil in
Wednesday
Between 8 and 10

Psalms of Brujas 9

"Docile"

I will not be docile
Or quiet
Because one fears my Black
Nor will I unhem my skirt
Because one can not control their cravings for sweet nectar
I will not choke back my truths
At the risk of asphyxiation
So that others remain in comfort

I have straightened my own back
Bend only on my own terms

Crosses

My name is not Jesus
Nor Christ
So please pack up your crucifixes
I will not pay your sins in my flesh
Nor sacrifice it to
Caress your palate

I would rather be a slave
With the station of a slave

Than to be a slave
Adored as king

My breasts are empty
Tears dry
With only enough blood to save myself
I can not teach you to be fierce, strong or savvy
For I have been none of those things
And can not comfort you in your disappointment when you realize
Your assumptions were wrong
I won't be sold
Traded
Paraded
Used as justification
Imitated
Replaced
Or resurrected

This beautiful Black being
Can no longer be your scapegoat

Your welfare-economy-crashing-target-practice-bearing breeder
Thot
Bop
Breezy
Bitch
Villain
Whipping-post-for-you
Mama-or-Daddy-issues

Only human
Only being
Only Black
Fragile
But resilient
Violent when necessary
And if you wanna see it
Touch my seed

Or stand somewhere between me
And my freedom

Survival is the only magic here

The rest is smoke and mirrors
Fueled by projected insecurity

See
We can all uncloak now

Stop choking on smoke now
Just be folks now

Say vulnerable shit like

"I can't do this on my own, could you help now?"

"I don't wanna be touched."

"This is how I need to be loved, it's 50/50 or nothing."

See what it's like to just breathe
Simply just be

Those crosses were heavy
Can't you feel the relief?

Peace

I wish
There was
Something
I could write
That would
Change
Their minds

Change the climate
And
Rewind time

I wish there were something
I could say
That would
Radiate like light to the young
Teaching them the lessons I've learned

Without the pain
Without polluted rain
Without the stinging sensation of hunger
Without the mishaps, setbacks and fumbles

I
Sigh sometimes
Cry sometimes
Find myself engulfed

In rage

More times that not
Stomach turned in knots
In a world full of not's

Wondering how we could
Not
Not
Be passive

Not
Fight
Not
Protest

Not
Riot

Not set this shit
On fire

All the while helping them tie the last
Knot on the noose
They intend to
Hang us with

I wish
There was something I could
Paint

Something I can
Make

A picture
I could take

A trigger I could pull

A button to push

A switch to flip

A clip to empty

To open the gates
That cage them

Resurrect them from graves that contain them
Release the chains that chain them
Retie the bonds that bind them
Undo the things that shame them
The hurt that pains them
The scars that remind them of
The things that aged them

Way beyond their years

Retract their tears
Conquer their fears
Fix that broken mirrors
Pick up their shattered pieces

So we can once again be whole

I wish there was some
Phrase we could call and respond

A magic wand
That would wave it all away

All the pain
All the brainwashing
And backward births
Our detachment from the earth

Our purpose
Ourselves
Our Gods

By the time that knot moved from my throat

And down to my stomach
All I could muster was

Peace

Fear

Hi,

We've been friends
For a while
And grown to know each other
Quite well
And in some ways you've served me

But if we're honest

You've kept me stagnant
Judgemental and mostly towards the ones I love
Self-doubting
Self-hating
Mistrusting
And suffocated
So here

Now

Is where
We unyoke

I have spoken
Peace and love in your place
Patience
Acceptance

And
Integrity
In your place

Though we both know you're not the type
To just leave when you're told
We also both know
That I am persistent

So listen

Dear Fear,

You are no longer welcome
This heart has no room for your scorn
For your forked tongue or ill wishes
Your self-destructive tendencies
Can no longer be my safety net
Or an excuse
So please excuse me
But
Here, old friend, is where we part.

Hell

We was born in hell
Amongst
Crack pipes
Rapists
And pistols

Most sat in cells
Before we could spell it
Including myself
And they wonder why
We reckless

Shit
Only thing left
Is Paradise
But I found
That antidote
To the sickness
And it's called
Organize

My people
Rise
Up

This coonery is not our nature
This land is not our home

The grave is a destination
And not your destiny

I cried too
Lied too

Wanted to die
Asked
But never got a justified
Answer for why

Post-traumatic stress disorder
Depression
Anger management
Prozac
Remedial classes
And
Purp
None of it worked
Until these invisible
Chains became tangible

You a slave
Fixed wages
Can you feed yourself
Clothe your babies
Write your own history
Can you defend your home
When the Big Bad Wolf comes blowin'

Or should we call 911

And hope
Our faces don't
End up
Stenciled on
Picket signs

Or our names chanted
Onto the deaf ears

Of slave catchers
Casket chasers
And opportunists

Untitled

Badges
Bars
Batons

Broken
Bones

Bastard
Babies

Daddies
Stolen

Bloody
Mattresses

Black
Body
Mountains

Topped
By
Blue
Lines

Flags
Flying

Fear
Mongering

Subjective
Safety
Sold

To whoever has enough dexterity to dial 911

X Millennials

Those of us
Born in the cusp
Of Generation X'ers and Millennials

Those of us indoctrinated
To believe that a college education would save us

And the instant realization

That it wasn't enough

We are youthful enough to throw molotovs
And grown enough to ignore the consequences

Death on
Death on
Death
Death

Blessed on
Blessed on
Blessed
Blessed

We indigo
Gamma rays

Intellectually woke
Psychologically stunted
And physically numb

We had analog childhoods
Digitally adulting

We
Don't
Carry
Cash
Except for that emergency money
Tucked in paperback books
We still read

Psalms of Brujas 6:1

Speak up they say
Tell us your truth

Be brave
You're amazing

Fucking resilient

But the memories live in our bones
In our wombs
In the soil
Like hot sandy beaches
Generations of us
Are still dusting the sand from our feet
With the stitch of ocean, feces, and after birth
Still lingering in our noses

Born here
Born here

But we are not Cracker Jack box prizes
Disguised as cheap labor

Born here

Psalms of Brujas 6:2

Not born here
My mama had a home birth on Pluto
My nursery rhymes
Contained harsh criticisms
And frequent reminders
Of greatness
Neither can be forgotten

Follow Me

Follow me, she said
I got somethin' to show you
Somethin' you never seen befo'
It fit like a glove
Belongs to you
Even if you don't believe it exists

Despite your intuition
Tellin' you it do

Listen, she said
Be grateful for tomorrow's blessings
Today
As if they had come the day befo'
And watch your intentions
Bare more fruit than your arms
Can stand to hold

Follow me, she whispered

So I did

She lead me to a river
Showed me a reflection
It was the view from my grandmother's womb

I could hear the voices

All begging to be born

And me quietly knowing
All the while
That I was the one

She asked me where did that fire go
I told her I didn't know

But we both knew

That we both knew

But wouldn't mention it
Cause there's certain things
You just shouldn't say

So she showed me
How to soak those seeds in salty tears
And return them both back to the earth where they belong

So the silence could stop choking my roots
So pain could stop stripping away bark leaving me exposed
So blossoms would grow
Where brittle branches once were

So that the trees destined
To grow in my shade
Wouldn't suffer the same fate
So when they open their mouths
The voices that came out would be their own

And the ones they choked on

Would be the ones they choose

Follow me, she said
She had something to show me
Something I've seen before
It fit me like a glove
It belonged to me
Always had been mine
And mine alone

Mandate

Cast votes
Slit throats
Grow food

Grow

Consult our ancestors
Teach the babies

Run
For something
Office
Fences
Gates
Borders
Something

Sing
God dammit keep singing
Paint
Spray cans
Brushes
Or apps

Write
Poems
Rhymes

Think pieces
Provoking posts
All of it

Learn to shoot
Get a gun
Make bullets
Teach your babies
How and when to use them
There is nothing more dangerous
Than a fascist regime
And an unarmed population

Think
Critically
Question
Critique
For clarity
Not shame or superiority
Principal over popularity or peace

Listen
To yourself
What's not being said

Body language
Tone and cadence

Be patient
And if you can't
Then don't

Just go

God dammit just go
               And godspeed

Remember, leave a path
So others can follow

Heal
Us
Them
And
Those to come

Pray if you must
Just don't forget
To get up

There will come a time
When the best thing to do
Is nothing
So
Do nothing

Rest
Breathe deeply
Again

Mourn
Take the time to grieve

Bury your loved ones

Not the pain
Scream
Cry

Or don't
Just do it

Yes,
And fuck
Make love
To whomever you make love to
How ever you do it
Fuck them like
They have oxygen
And
You need it.

Make magic, babies, or at the very least an orgasm

Find it

That thing
The thing time has no hold on
Keeps you up at night

Resist
Any and everything
In the way of your

Of
Our Freedom
As, they are connected.

reading guide

Theme: LOVE

We commonly think of love as a feeling or an attachment. Love itself has no beginning or end, it just is and exists in many forms. One can love a person, a place, an experience, or an object. Love can also be transactional in nature, "If you love me then you will ....." which implies love is also an action or actionable. Meaning we can act because of love or "out of love". The first section of *Love, Lyric & Liberation* explores love from several vantage points, romantic love, love of self, love of culture and people.

Prompt(s):

- Identify 2–3 examples of where love, the "feeling," and love, the "action," intersect. For example, we see in "Cages" that maternal love inspires these women to create road maps to freedom for their children, even though their physical bodies are caged.
- What actions have you taken that were inspired by love?
- Who or what was that object of that love?
- Was that love reciprocated? If not, was reciprocation possible or necessary?

Theme: LYRIC

As a Black Woman of African descent, many of my cultural traditions are passed down via oration. When faced with a dilemma or in moments of joy, things my elders said to me, songs, poems saying have never failed to embody whatever feeling is at bay. We know that "sticks and stones" hurt and so do words. Words have the ability to conjure feelings, bring revelations, offer support or abandonment.

The "Lyric" section of *Love, Lyric, and Liberation* is an offering and tribute to our elders' wise words, to the MC's clever metaphors, the poet's meticulous placement of words, and the storyteller's tone and inflection.

Prompt(s):

- Create 1–2 proverbs inspired by a poem in the "Lyric" section of *Love, Lyric, and Liberation*.
- (a proverb is a short witty saying which states a general truth or offers a piece of advice.)

Example: *Shame is heavier than sin and trauma combined* (poem: "Psalms of Brujas 2")

Theme: LIBERATION

In the context above, to liberate or engage in liberation means to free oneself/collective from a state of oppression.

Most intuitively, know that we are not "free" people. Fewer of us have an intellectual understanding of who or what is oppressing us. I dare to say, most if not all of us are still attempting to understand what or who "we" are outside the identities assigned to us by our oppressors. This section of *Love, Lyric, and Liberation* explores the state of being oppressed and the mechanism we need and have access to in order to free ourselves.

Prompt(s):

- What stands between you and your liberation?
- Are you able to name/identify "the oppressed" and "the oppressor " in the lyric section. *(Hint: think outside the box. Some of the "opressors" and the "oppressed" in these pieces are literal, figurative, or both. In the poem "West," the figurative oppressor is the wind while the literal oppressor is the Trans-Atlantic Slave Trade.)*

acknowledgments

I would like to show gratitude to my mother, her mother, her mother, and all their mothers. Thank you for living and giving life.

A special thank you to Nomadic Press and its staff for seeing my vision and bringing it to life.

Michaela...Thank you for helping me translate the voice into the words on these pages. J. K., I have deep gratitude for your patience. Thank you for not telling me that I was buggin' because I most definitely was.

To my "A-1's and Day-1's," Jesse, Tinker, and Sheree. I am because you are.

Alma and Troy, there are many lessons you taught me and I am grateful.

To all the Black men who loved me, held me, and kept me safe, I love you: Turha, Che, Uncle Jamie, Uncle Vester, Uncle Roddy, Uncle Eric, Uncle Donald, Uncle Robbie, Dad, Grandpa, Robert, Micheal, CJ, and Adam. Thank you.

For my sisters in arms, Cat and Carroll, thank you for all you give, for loving me and us beyond measure. If the wind is at your back, know that I will be by your side.

For all my nieces and nephews, blood and chosen, watching y'all grow has been the joy of my life and you forever inspire me.

Breanna, I still wanna be like you when I grow up.

Baba Jahsun Edmonds, thank you for your wisdom, guidance, and prayers. May the creator continue to bless you as you bless the people.

To the rest of my loved ones, comrades, colleagues, and fellow freedom fighters: Thank you for serving the people. Thank you for believing in us and me even when I didn't have the gumption to believe in myself.

To my children: Aryana, Athena, and Ajani. Thank you for choosing me.

CJ, my dear, our bond is beyond words and worlds. I love you.

Robert Boykin, Our mother is proud. *KICK PUSH!*

Adam, I could have never done this without you. Your love, support, talent, and beauty has made me a better person. Thank you will never be enough.

I pray these words heal whoever reads them.

Thank you to the following publications, in which some of these poems, in earlier forms, previously appeared: "Psalms of Brujas 11: Pussy" in *Tofu Ink*; "Psalms of Brujas 3" in *805 Lit*; and "Sirus P" as video by Jaded Ibis for *SoFloPoJo* (*South Florida Poetry Journal*).

Asantewaa Boykin, R.N.

Asantewaa Boykin, R.N, M.I.C.N, is the daughter of Valerie Boykin, grand-daughter of Bertha Brandy and Gladys Boykin, and the great-granddaughter of Nonnie Boykin and Drucella Bluford. She is a proud San Diego, California, native who found her voice in Oakland, California. Her poetry combines a love of words, storytelling, and resistance, which explores topics such as space travel, Black-femme militancy, and motherhood. Boykin is a co-founder of APTP (Anti Police-Terror Project), an organization committed to the eradication of police terror in all forms. She uses her knowledge of nursing and activism to provide street medic training for direct actions and community training on trauma-centered first aid. She is also a founding member of the Capital City Black Nurses Association. Boykin, along with a brave group of organizers and medical professionals, developed Mental Health First (or MH First), a mobile response team aimed at minimizing police contact with those who are in the midst of mental health crises. Her greatest honor is being the mother of son Ajani, bonus daughter Aryana, and granddaughter Lilith.

Nomadic Press Emergency Fund

Nomadic Press Black Writers Fund

Right before Labor Day 2020 (and in response to the effects of COVID), Nomadic Press launched its Emergency Fund, a forever fund meant to support Nomadic Press-published writers who have no income, are unemployed, don't qualify for unemployment, have no healthcare, or are just generally in need of covering unexpected or impactful expenses.

Funds are first come, first serve, and are available as long as there is money in the account, and there is a dignity centered internal application that interested folks submit. Disbursements are made for any amount up to $300.

All donations made to this fund are kept in a separate account. The Nomadic Press Emergency Fund (NPEF) account and associated processes (like the application) are overseen by Nomadic Press authors and the group meets every month.

On Juneteenth (June 19) 2020, Nomadic Press launched the Nomadic Press Black Writers Fund (NPBWF), a forever fund that will be directly built into the fabric of our organization for as long as Nomadic Press exists and puts additional monies directly into the pockets of our Black writers at the end of each year.

Here is how it works:

$1 of each book sale goes into the fund.

At the end of each year, all Nomadic Press authors have the opportunity to voluntarily donate none, part, or all of their royalties to the fund.

Anyone from our larger communities can donate to the fund. This is where you come in!

At the end of the year, whatever monies are in the fund will be evenly distributed to all Black Nomadic Press authors that have been published by the date of disbursement (mid-to-late December).

The fund (and associated, separate bank account) has an oversight team comprised of four authors (Ayodele Nzinga, Daniel B. Summerhill, Dazié Grego-Sykes, and Odelia Younge) + Nomadic Press Executive Director J. K. Fowler.

Please consider supporting these funds. You can also more generally support Nomadic Press by donating to our general fund via nomadicpress.org/donate and by continuing to buy our books. As always, thank you for your support!

Scan the QR code for more information and/or to donate.

You can also donate at nomadicpress.org/store.